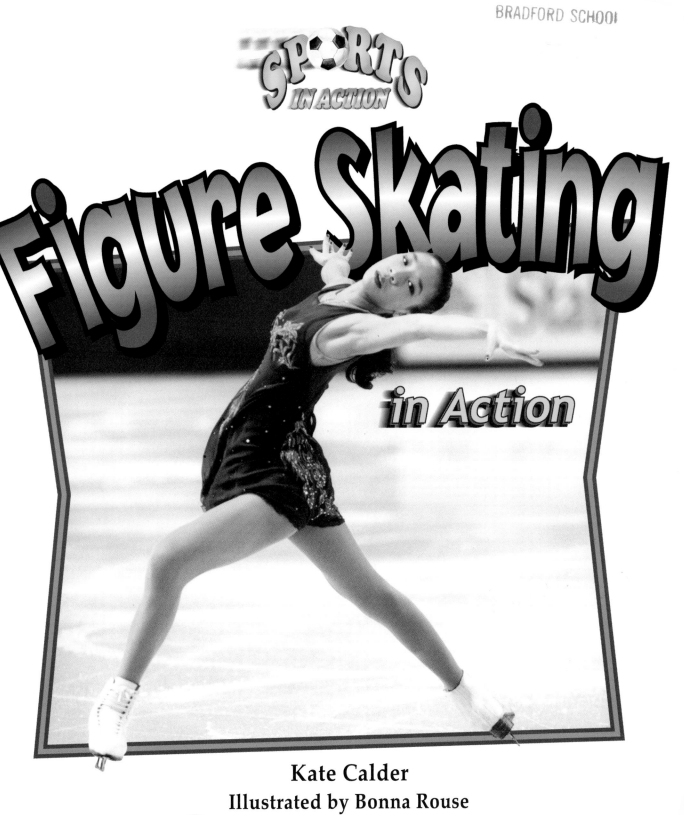

SPORTS IN ACTION

Figure Skating

in Action

Kate Calder

Illustrated by Bonna Rouse

Crabtree Publishing Company

www.crabtreebooks.com

Created by Bobbie Kalman

For Liane Bacal and Sari Stulberg
—skaters

Editor-in-Chief
Bobbie Kalman

Author
Kate Calder

Managing editor
Lynda Hale

Editors
Niki Walker
John Crossingham
Hannelore Sotzek
Amanda Bishop

Computer design
Lynda Hale
Kate Calder

Photo researcher
Kate Calder

Production coordinator
Hannelore Sotzek

Illustrations
Bonna Rouse

Special thanks to
Gillian Marie Grogan, Mila Kirstie Kulsa, Linda Lester-Koplar,
Alexandra Porcu

Consultant
Karen Cover, World Figure Skating Museum, Colorado Springs, Colorado

Photographs
Nancie Battaglia Photography: pages 30-31; Bruce Curtis: pages 7, 10, 12, 13,
14, 16 (bottom), 17, 19 (top three), 20; Image Communications/Scott Grant:
pages 6, 21, 24; Photos On Ice/Michelle Harvath: pages 3, 4, 11, 19 (bottom),
22, 23 (right), 25 (bottom), 28-29; Photos On Ice/Paul Harvath: front cover,
title page, 5 (top), 23 (left), 25 (top), 26, 27 (both); SportsChrome: page 18;
Bob Tringali/SportsChrome: page 16 (top); The World Figure Skating Museum:
page 5 (bottom)

Every reasonable effort has been made in obtaining authorization, where
necessary, to publish images of the athletes who appear in this book. The
publishers would be pleased to have any oversights or omissions brought
to their attention so that they may be corrected for subsequent printings.

Digital prepress
Embassy Graphics

Printer
Worzalla Publishing Company

Crabtree Publishing Company

www.crabtreebooks.com   1-800-387-7650

PMB 16A
350 Fifth Avenue,
Suite 3308
New York, NY
10118

612 Welland Avenue
St. Catharines,
Ontario
Canada
L2M 5V6

73 Lime Walk
Headington,
Oxford
OX3 7AD
United Kingdom

Cataloging-in-Publication Data
Calder, Kate
   Figure skating in action

p. cm. — (Sports in action)
Includes index.

ISBN 0-7787-0165-4 (library bound) — ISBN 0-7787-0177-8 (pbk.)
This book introduces the techniques and equipment of figure skating,
as well as ice dancing, pair skating, and synchronized skating.

1. Skating—Juvenile literature. [1. Ice skating.] I. Rouse, Bonna, ill.
II. Title. III. Series: Kalman, Bobbie. Sports in action.

GV850.4 .C35 2001   j796.91'2—dc21   LC 00-057078
                                                                    CII

Contents

What is Figure Skating?

Figure skating is a sport that combines athletics and art. Skaters perform **programs**, or routines, that are made up of different jumps, spins, and artistic dance movements. Individuals, pairs, or groups of skaters compete against one another. Judges award points to skaters based on the difficulty and originality of their program.

Competitions

Figure skaters of all ages participate in competitions held by local skating clubs. Many skaters dream of competing in a national figure skating competition. They must first compete and win a medal in a series of competitions to earn a spot in a national championship. Winners of these national events advance to compete against skaters from other countries at the World Figure Skating Championships. Winners of a national competition may also get the chance to compete in the Winter Olympics, which are held every four years.

*Competitive figure skating has four **disciplines**, or categories, in which skaters practice and compete —**mens singles**, **ladies singles**, **pairs**, and **ice dance**. This skater is competing in the ladies singles event. Turn to pages 24 and 26 to learn more about pairs and ice dance.*

How it began

Skating began hundreds of years ago in Northern Europe as a means of traveling on frozen rivers, lakes, and canals. Over time, skating became a popular leisure activity. In the 1600s the king of England tried skating, and soon the sport became even more popular. Skaters in Britain began doing fancy moves and jumps on skates. In France, people began adding spins and new steps to make skating more artistic. It was not long before skating became popular during the cold winters in North America.

The first skates were boots that had bones strapped to their soles. Eventually, skates were improved by replacing bone blades with metal ones, as found on skates today.

Why is it called "figure" skating?

Figure skating got its name from the **figures**, or designs, that skaters traced on the ice with their blades, as shown left. In early competitions, skaters were judged on these intricate figures. Over time, skaters began adding graceful movements to their tracings. Eventually, they skated to music and incorporated dancelike movements into a routine. Competitions had two events—a series of figures with set patterns traced on the ice and a **freestyle** routine with jumps and spins performed to music. Skaters no longer perform figures in competition

The Essentials

A pair of figure skates and an icy surface are all you really need to practice skating skills. Many communities have an indoor ice **rink**, or skating surface. You can practice skills on your own or take lessons. Most rinks are open only during the skating season, which is from September to June.

Dress warmly in layers of clothing. You can take off layers as your body gets warm.

Gloves or mittens keep a skater's hands warm and protect them if he or she falls. Most skaters do not wear gloves during a competition.

Blades need to be sharpened by a professional. Most rinks have **a pro shop** where blades can be sharpened.

Women often wear tights with leggings or skating dresses. Most men wear athletic pants or leggings.

All figure-skate blades have **toe picks** that allow the skater to perform jumps and spins.

Skates

Figure skates must be sturdy enough to prevent your ankles from leaning inward. Figure-skating boots are made of several layers of tough leather. The heel has an added layer called the **counter** to provide extra support. Your skates should fit snugly so that your heel cannot slide up and down inside the boot. You can injure your ankles by wearing skates that are flimsy or loose on your feet. When trying on skates, wear the socks and tights that you plan to wear when you skate.

When you finish skating, dry your blades with a towel. Put a soft cover around each blade to keep it from scratching or cutting the other skate. When you get home, undo the laces to allow the inside of the boots to dry.

Coaches

Advanced figure skaters need a coach to teach them proper techniques. Coaches help skaters with their jumps and spins. They also attend competitions. The coaches help prepare the skaters before they step on the ice to skate their program.

Guards

Guards protect your blades when you are not on the ice. Wear your guards even on rubber flooring because dirt on the floor can damage your blades. Rinse your guards often so that they are free of any dirt, which will dull your blades.

Warming Up

Figure skating uses a lot of different muscles that may cramp or pull if they are not stretched properly. Everyone falls on the ice sometime. Stretching before you skate reduces the risk of bruising or tearing your muscles when you fall. Before stretching, skip rope or do jumping jacks to warm up your muscles so they stretch more easily.

Neck stretch

Tilt your head forward so that your chin points down at your chest. Slowly roll your head to one shoulder and then the other. Never roll your head backward! You might injure the bones in your neck.

Trunk circles

Stand with your feet shoulder-width apart and rotate your waist in a large circle. Keep your shoulders as still as possible.

Arm circles

Slowly swing your arms in large circles, making the circles smaller until your arms are straight out to your sides. Now reverse the direction, starting with small circles and ending with giant ones.

Front lunges

Stretching your hips helps prevent
back injuries. To do a front lunge,
bend your leg forward and keep
your other leg straight. Hold for
a count of ten and switch legs.

Side lunges

Stand with your feet facing forward
and spread them as far apart as
you can. Bend one knee and
lean to that side. Rest your
hands on your bent knee
for balance. Count to
fifteen and then
slowly straighten
up. Repeat the
stretch on the
opposite side.

Thigh stretch

Hold onto the boards with one hand
to keep your balance. Stand on your
right foot and bring your left foot up
behind you. Grab your foot and pull
it gently until you feel the stretch in
the front of your leg. Hold for a count
of ten and switch legs.

On the Edge

Skaters use the edges of their blades to push themselves with every step they take. Skating on the edge of your blade allows you to turn in a circle or curve. Being able to glide on an **outside edge** or an **inside edge** will give your strides strength and speed. Having a good understanding of edges is important for learning how to spin and to take off when jumping.

Skaters practice their edges by skating around a circle or a half circle. This skater is practicing her edges.

(inset) Skating on an edge creates a crisp tracing on the ice.

Outside and Inside

The bottom of a blade has a slight hollow curve, creating two edges on either side— the inside edge and the outside edge. The inside edge of your blade faces in toward your other foot. Your outside edge faces out from your foot. Practice shifting your blade from outside to inside while standing on the ice.

The toe pick has five points for digging into the ice.

The outside ridge of the blade is called the outside edge. The inside edge is the ridge along the inside of the blade.

The hollow curve begins at the toe pick and extends to the back of the blade.

Staying on the edge

You must have control of your body position in order to **hold**, or stay balanced on, an edge. If you are skating on your right leg, then this leg is your **skating leg** and the right side of your body is your **skating side**. By keeping your skating side firm and strong, you will have the control you need to perform movements with grace and ease.

*This skater is skating on a **deep**, or very angled, outside edge. She has to keep her skating leg and skating side strong to hold the position.*

Smooth Skating

Keeping your balance while moving on the ice can be tricky at first! Learn to keep your back straight and knees bent. This position will help keep you from losing your balance. Keeping your knees bent also makes it easier to shift your weight from leg to leg as you skate across the ice. The leg on which you place your weight is your skating leg. The other leg is called your **free leg**.

Pushing off

To start moving on the ice, you have to **push off** with your skates. The **T-push off**, shown left, is the easiest push off to learn. With your arms at waist height and your knees slightly bent, arrange your feet like a capital "T." The front foot points forward, and the back foot points to the side. Bend your knees, lean forward slightly, and push with your back foot.

Gliding

Gliding is moving smoothly across the ice while keeping your body still. Beginners first learn to glide forward on both blades. Start with a T-push off and glide as far as you can. When you are comfortable gliding on two feet, try lifting one foot off the ice. As you lift your free leg, keep your weight on your skating leg and your arms at waist height for balance.

To do a T-push off, use the inside edge of your blade—not your toe pick. Straighten your leg behind you as you push off.

Stroking

When you are comfortable gliding on one foot, you are ready to try **stroking**. Stroking allows you to continue moving without needing to stop and do a T-push off. Stroking is a little like walking—while one foot is on the ice, you lift the other foot to move your body forward. Just before you lift each foot, push off to the side and slightly backward with your blade.

(right) To perfect your stroking, push off onto a forward outside edge with every step.

Just wiggle

The easiest way to skate backward is to stand with your feet shoulder-width apart and your knees slightly bent. Now wiggle your hips back and forth. Twisting your body and turning your feet from side to side will get you moving backward slowly. You can also try moving backward by pushing both feet out and then bringing them together at the same time. This move is called **double sculling** or a **wizzle**. It makes an hourglass pattern on the ice.

When you are comfortable wiggling backward, try stroking backward. Push one leg forward and off the ice and then the other.

Stops

Now that you can skate, you need to know how to stop properly. Use the side of your blade to slow down either gradually or quickly. The three most popular stopping movements in figure skating are the **hockey stop**, **snowplow**, and **T-stop**.

Hockey stop

When skaters need to stop fast, they use the hockey stop, as shown above. To do a hockey stop, quickly twist your whole body sideways. Push your blades forward and downward into the ice. Your blades will skid to a stop.

The snowplow

Most beginners learn to stop using the snowplow. To snowplow, gradually turn your toes toward one another so that your feet make a "V." Your blades will resemble the front of a snowplow, and you may even build a little pile of "snow" in front of you as you stop.

T-stop

The T-stop uses the same foot positions as the T-push off. Arrange your feet in a "T," shift your weight to your back leg, and skid to a stop. Lean back far enough so that you are able to skid on an outside edge. Be careful not to step on the back of the blade that is gliding forward. You could fall instead of stopping!

Directions

Figure skating involves turning and skating in different directions. Being able to turn and skate around curves helps you perform advanced figure skating moves.

Crossovers

Crossovers allow you to skate in a curve with speed and control. To curve to the left, extend your right arm in front of you and your left arm behind you. This position will help you lean into the curve. Cross your right foot over your left leg and place it on the ice. Now lift your left leg and step forward with it. Keep crossing over until you curve as far as you like. As you become better at crossovers, try building up speed by pushing off with each leg as you lift it from the ice.

Lean into the curve, as shown above, to gain speed as you do crossovers.

Turning backward

Sometimes you will want to switch from forward to backward skating. A **three turn** allows you to make this change. Simply shift your weight from a front outside edge to a backward inside edge. Use your arms and upper body to twist into the turn.

Glide forward and rotate your upper body. This winding motion will help you begin the turn. To make the turn, stop rotating your upper body inward and pull it in the opposite direction.

Back crossovers

Back crossovers are similar to front crossovers, but they require more practice to master.

1. To curve to the right, extend your right arm behind you as you glide backward. Watch the direction in which you are skating.

2. Cross your left foot over and in front of your right leg and place it on the ice. Now lift your right leg and place it to your right, as shown in step 1. To gain speed, push off the ice with each skate as you lift it off the ice. Remember to lean into the curve.

Spinning

The best spinners can spin at high speeds without moving an inch across the ice! Skaters spin on the inside edges of their blade and usually move in a counter-clockwise direction. Start with a two-foot spin to get used to the spinning motion. Twist your arms to the right and then quickly swing them to the left. Point your toes inward slightly and spin on the inside edges of your blade.

*The **layback** can be the most difficult spin in which to stay balanced. To make your layback unique, hold your free leg and your arms in different positions.*

Scratch spin

1. Learning a **scratch spin**, or **corkscrew**, takes practice. To begin a scratch spin, do several back crossovers and hold the final crossover so that you create a large circle on your back inside edge.

2. Step forward into the circle and then do a three turn from a forward edge to a backward edge to help you start spinning. Keep your skating leg bent and your free leg and both arms out to the side.

3. After you make the turn onto your inside edge, slowly straighten your skating leg and bring your other leg close to your body. Cross your arms tightly over your chest to help keep your balance.

Many spins

Once you have mastered the scratch spin, you are ready to try spins with advanced body positions. The **sit spin**, shown right, is done in a crouched, sitting position with your free leg extended in front. In a **camel spin**, your leg is extended straight behind your body. Some skaters make a camel or sit spin even more difficult by changing the leg on which they are spinning in the middle of the spin. They also combine many positions together in one spin, such as going from a camel position into a layback position and then down into a sit position.

Jumping

Jumping is the most difficult aspect of figure skating. A skater uses speed to gain the momentum needed to leap off the ice and rotate in the air. There are two main types of jumps—taking off from an edge and taking off from a toe pick. For an **edge jump**, bend your takeoff leg deeply to create force for springing up into the air. To perform a **toe jump**, use your toe pick as leverage to pop up off the ice. The **waltz** is an edge jump and is one of the easiest jumps to master.

The waltz jump

1. Begin on a forward outside edge and keep your knee bent.

2. Swing your arms and legs in front of you and spring up off your knee.

This skater has just used her right toe pick to pop up off the ice into a jump.

Split jumps

A **split jump**, shown left, is not performed to rotate in the air but rather to show a split position in the air. The skater uses his or her toe pick to leap into the air with one leg stretched forward and the other stretched behind. In a **Russian split jump**, the skater brings one leg up to each side.

Split jumps do not earn as many points as other jumps, but they are spectacular to watch.

3. Keep your arms close to your chest and make a half-turn in the air.

4. Once you are facing the other direction, land softly with a bent knee.

5. Extend your leg back and arms forward for a strong, balanced landing position.

All Together

Figure skating is more than just jumps and spins. Skaters add elegant dance movements and steps to create a graceful program. Programs last from one minute to four-and-a-half minutes, depending on the skater's skill level. Skaters usually wear elaborate outfits for competitions. The costumes suit the music or theme of the program. Most skaters have their costumes made especially for them.

Spirals

Spirals are long, graceful moves in which you glide on an edge, while fully extending your free leg and leaning forward so that your body is parallel to the ice. The key to making a great spiral is raising your free leg high behind you. Practice a spiral position while holding onto the boards. Rest your palms on the boards in front of you, lower your chest, and raise your free leg behind you. Have a partner check to make sure that your free leg is straight and your toe is turned slightly to the side.

*In top competitions, skaters must do a series of spirals called a **spiral sequence**. They change from front to back spirals and use different arm movements and leg positions.*

Footwork

Footwork is a series of quick, eye-catching turns and foot movements. Skaters are marked on the difficulty of their steps and movements. Footwork can move across the ice in a straight line, large circle, or S-shaped pattern. Three turns, **mohawks**, small hops, and lunges are just some of the steps that can be included in footwork.

In order to show off a wide range of skills and creativity, skaters use more than one style of music in their program. The songs change about midway through the program, allowing the skater to switch from fast, upbeat moves to slow, graceful ones

*(left) A skater's toes point outward to perform a **spread eagle** around a curve.*

Pair Skating

Pair skating is the most dangerous and difficult type of figure skating. A male and female skate together and perform jumps and spins in **unison**, or at the same time. Pair skaters must have excellent timing to execute jumps and lifts. Partners must also have a lot of trust in each other!

Jumps

Skaters must be strong, consistent jumpers to perform with a partner. Both skaters have to time and control their jumps perfectly. When making side-by-side jumps, the pair must leave the ice and land at the same time. A **throw jump** is a spectacular jump in which the man throws the woman into the jump position. The woman has to practice landing with a lot of force and speed.

In pair skating, the man is usually a larger and stronger skater than the woman in order to support her during lifts and throws.

Lifts

There are several pair lifts. They take a great amount of practice, skill, strength, and instruction from a professional coach. In the one-hand **lasso lift**, shown right, the skaters start face to face. At the top of the lift, the woman turns her body to face the same direction as that of the man. The man then releases one hand and supports the woman with one arm only.

Spins

Pair skaters perform **solo spins**, which are done side by side, and **pair spins**, in which the skaters spin together. In solo spins, the partners must begin the spin in unison and time their rotations perfectly. One skater calls out when it is time to end the spin. Pair spins can be done in any basic position such as the **pair-camel spin** and the **pair-sit spin**. In the pair-sit spin, the man spins in a regular sit position while holding onto the woman, who spins on a backward edge.

*(top) The **death spiral** is the most thrilling pair spin. The woman leans back so that her head almost touches the ice. Why do you think it is called a death spiral?*

(right) Pair skaters try to perform movements and spins that are original and difficult. The two skaters do not have to be in the same position during a pair spin, as these skaters demonstrate.

Ice Dancing

Ice dancing looks like ballroom dancing on skates. Skaters perform dances such as waltzes and tangos. Each move must be exact. Partners skate close together and have to dance in unison. Every young ice dancer learns a series of dances with set patterns and steps that are outlined by the **International Skating Union**, or **ISU**.

Holds

Ice dancers use a variety of dance positions. The most common is the **waltz hold**, in which the skaters face each other. One partner skates forward, and the other skates backward. In the **foxtrot hold**, the bodies of the skaters face each other but both skaters move either backward or forward. In the **killian hold**, the man skates behind the woman. He holds her left hand outstretched and her right hand on her hip. The woman skates slightly in front of the man.

Ice dancers skate as close together as possible and are almost always touching. The partners try to look as though they are a single unit.

Dance competitions

Ice dance competitions are made up of three events—**compulsory dances**, an **original dance**, and a **freedance**. Every dance team performs the same two compulsory dances. These compulsory dances are chosen randomly from a series of dances outlined by the ISU. The original dance also has a set pattern, but the movements are arranged by the skaters themselves. The competitors repeat the pattern of the original dance twice during their performance.

These ice dancers are in a waltz hold. They are performing a compulsory dance.

Free-for-all!

The freedance is the final event and is created entirely by the skating team. The partners choose the theme and style of the freedance, which often has non-traditional movements and dance steps.

Freedance programs are usually flashy and fun. This team is ready to entertain the audience and judges with their performance.

Synchronized Skating

Synchronized skating is the newest figure skating event and is becoming extremely popular. Teams of skaters perform programs set to music. They create formations that look like patterns moving across the ice. These formations include circles, lines, and pinwheels. Skaters move smoothly from one formation to another.

Synchronized skating is a team effort. The skaters help one another through the program and make sure that their own movements match those of everyone else. If a skater falls during competition, it may cause another teammate to fall as well. Teams must practice a plan of recovery in case a skater falls during a competition.

This synchronized skating team is performing a **pinwheel**. *Several lines of skaters are rotating around a fixed spot in the middle—just like the spokes of a wheel. This pinwheel has six spokes, but some have as few as two.*

Ice Shows

Many skating clubs put on ice shows at the end of the skating season. The skaters wear costumes and perform in theatrical group programs. Ice shows offer a chance for skaters to show off their skills to the community and have a lot of fun.

Skaters spend hours learning and rehearsing the programs. On the night before the ice show, they have a dress rehearsal. In this practice, the skaters do a complete run-through of the show while wearing their costumes and make-up.

On the day of the show, the rink is decorated with props, lights, and banners. A giant curtain is hung across the ice at one side of the rink. "Backstage," or behind the curtain, the skaters get ready to perform. The arena is dark except for giant spotlights that illuminate the skaters on the ice. The skaters' families and friends fill the stands and cheer as the skaters take the ice.

These skaters are performing in a 1950s routine. Remember to smile and have fun in an ice show!

Figure Skating Words

crossovers Continuous steps in which one foot is crossed repeatedly over the other

discipline A type of figure skating, such as pairs, in which skaters practice and perform

edge jump A jump in which a skater leaps into the air from one foot

edges The outer ridges of the blade on which the skater skates; the act of skating on a blade's edge

inside edge The inner edge of the blade that faces in toward the other foot

landing position A position after a jump in which the free leg and arms are extended and controlled

mohawk A turn in which a skater steps from a forward inside edge on one foot to a backward inside edge on the opposite foot

outside edge The outer edge of the blade

program A set routine that a skater performs in competition

scratch spin A spin in which a skater rotates on one foot

side-by-side jumps A pair jump in which both skaters perform the same jump simultaneously

tango A traditional ballroom dance that includes quick, dramatic steps and movements

toe jump A jump in which a skater digs his or her toe pick into the ice to gain height

two-foot spin A spin in which a skater rotates on the inside edges of both skates on the ice

waltz A traditional ballroom dance that includes long edges and lilting steps

Index

1 2 3 4 5 6 7 8 9 0 Printed in the U.S.A. 9 8 7 6 5 4 3 2 1 0